JUPITER

PLANETS IN OUR SOLAR SYSTEM

CHILDREN'S ASTRONOMY EDITION

Jupiter is the fifth

planet from the Sun.

Jupiter is
the largest
in the Solar
System, more
than 1300
Earths could
fit inside it.

Jupiter is the fastest spinning planet in the Solar System.

Jupiter is a
gas giant with
a mass more
than 300 times
the mass of
the Earth.

Jupiter has the
shortest day of
all the planets.

Jupiter has a diameter of 142,750 kilometres.

Jupiter has three
very faint rings.

Jupiter is about 777 million kilometres away from the Sun.

Jupiter orbits the
Sun once every
11.8 Earth years.

Jupiter is
primarily
composed
of hydrogen
with a quarter
of its mass
being helium.

Jupiter's name came
from the Roman
god of mythology.

Jupiter has at least 67 moons, including the four large Galilean moons discovered by Galileo Galilei in 1610.

Jupiter's moon Ganymede is the largest moon in the solar system.

Jupiter has many storms raging on the surface, the great red spot is a huge storm that has been raging for over three hundred years.

Winds inside the
great red spot
storm reach speeds
of about 270 mph.

Jupiter is the
4th brightest
object in the
sky and was
known to
astronomers of
ancient times.

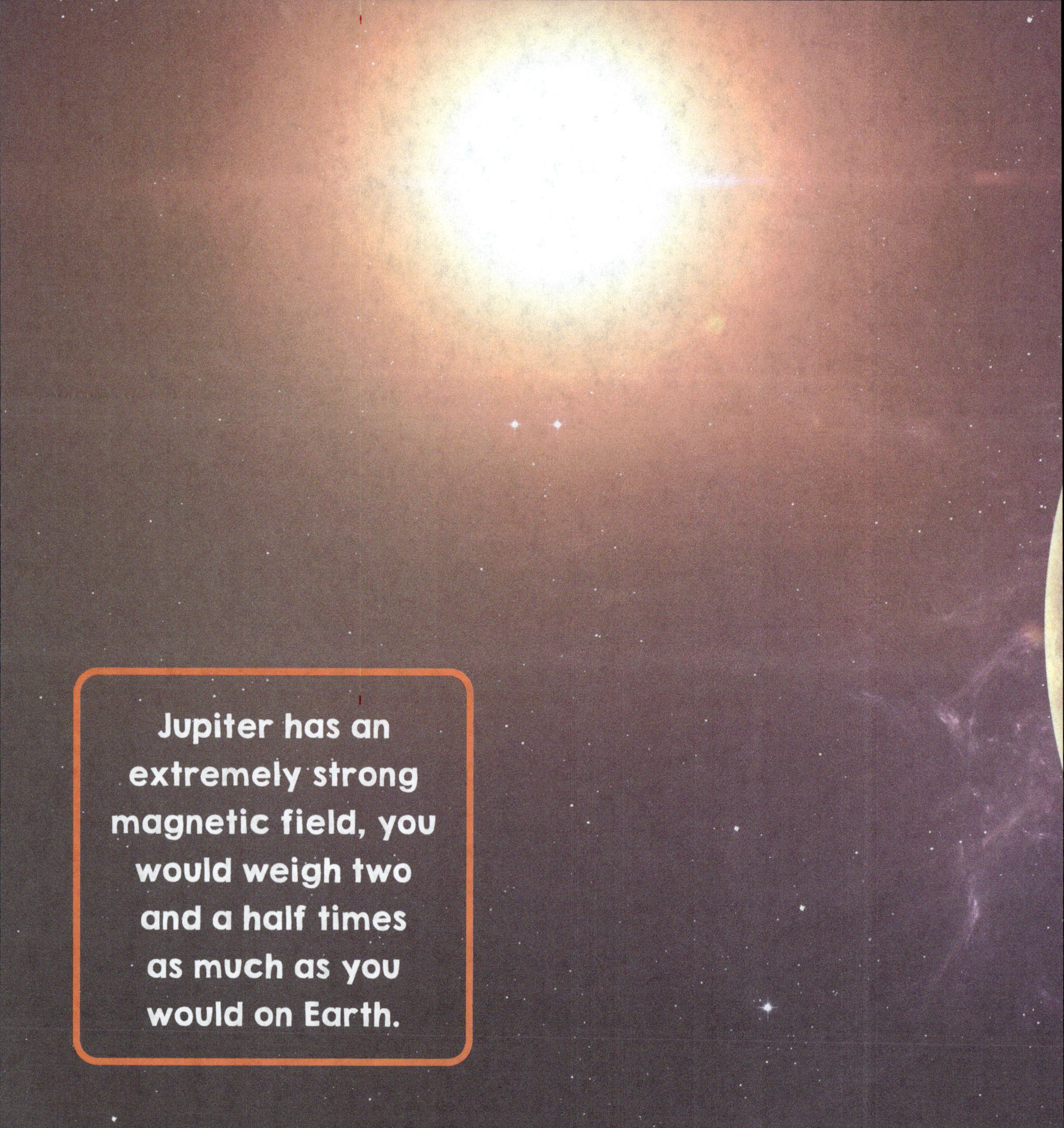

Jupiter has an
extremely strong
magnetic field, you
would weigh two
and a half times
as much as you
would on Earth.

Thick, colorful clouds of deadly poisonous gases surround Jupiter.

Jupiter has the largest planetary atmosphere in the Solar System.